Beyond the Sunset

Also by Kenneth W. Osbeck

25 Most Treasured Gospel Hymn Stories
52 Bible Characters Dramatized
52 Hymn Stories Dramatized
101 Hymn Stories
101 More Hymn Stories
Amazing Grace
Devotional Warm-Ups for the Church Choir
Hallelujah, What a Savior! (book and CD)
Joy to the World! (book and CD)
Ministry of Music
Pocket Guide to the Church Choir Member

Beyond the Sunset

25 Hymn Stories
Celebrating the Hope of Heaven

KENNETH W. OSBECK

kregel
PUBLICATIONS

Grand Rapids, MI 49501

Beyond the Sunset:
25 Hymn Stories Celebrating the Hope of Heaven

© 2001 by Kenneth W. Osbeck

Published by Kregel Publications, a division of Kregel, Inc., P.O. Box 2607, Grand Rapids, MI 49501. Kregel Publications provides trusted, biblical publications for Christian growth and service. Your comments and suggestions are valued. For more information about Kregel Publications, visit our web site: www.kregel.com.

ISBN 0-8254-3438-6

Printed in the United States of America

1 2 3 4 5 / 05 04 03 02 01

Contents

6 *Contents*

About the Author

Throughout a long career of teaching and directing music, Ken Osbeck has tried to lead Christians into a deeper understanding and appreciation of their church hymnal—next to the Bible itself, the most important book in one's relationship with God.

Since their retirement from teaching, Ken and his wife, Betty, have shared their dramatized hymn story and Bible character programs with more than five hundred church groups throughout the Midwest. God has greatly blessed the Osbecks' ministry, making it a spiritually enriching time in their lives. The Osbecks were formerly teachers in the Grand Rapids area at the Grand Rapids School of the Bible and Music and the Grand Rapids Baptist College and Seminary (now merged as Cornerstone University and Grand Rapids Baptist Seminary)—Ken in church music and the fine arts and Betty in speech and drama. They both hold graduate degrees from the University of Michigan. Ken has also served as music director in seven area churches and for the *Radio Bible Class, Children's Bible Hour,* and Youth for Christ. He is the author of a number of books for church music ministries, all published by Kregel Publications. The Osbecks are members of Calvary Church, Grand Rapids, Michigan, and have four grown children and two granddaughters.

Introduction

There is a land of pure delight, where saints immortal reign;
Infinite day excludes the night, and pleasures banish pain.

O! the delights, the heav'nly joys, the glories of the place,
Where Jesus sheds the brightest beams of His o'erflowing grace!

—*Isaac Watts*

Heaven is reserved for ransomed people. For all who have responded with personal faith to Christ's redemptive atonement, the Savior's promise of a glorious hereafter is as certain as God Himself, who "in the beginning . . . created the heavens and the earth" (Gen. 1:1).

*In my Father's house are many rooms. . . . I am going there to
prepare a place for you . . . that you also may be where I am.*

—John 14:2-3

Though God has provided much in this life for our welfare and happiness, the best that earth offers is merely a dim reflection of the perfection that awaits the child of God:

*No eye has seen, no ear has heard, no mind has conceived what
God has prepared for those who love him.*

—1 Corinthians 2:9

9

Biblical teaching about heaven has generally been neglected in the Christian church, possibly because the concepts of eternity are beyond our limited experience and expression. Who can adequately answer all of the questions about infinite time and space? Yet we can reflect on the truths that God reveals in the Scriptures. We should eagerly anticipate the prospect of worshiping and serving His risen, victorious Son.

A serious reflection about heaven will change our perception of this life, making us more aware of the brevity of our earthly years when compared with heaven's eternity (James 4:14). It will heighten our desire to live each moment with Christlike purity.

> *Everyone who has this hope in him purifies himself,*
> *just as he is pure.*
> —1 John 3:3

An important reminder of heaven's joys is the church hymnal. Helpful insights about the hereafter are found in many of our favorite hymns:

> When I draw my final breath, when my eyes shall close in death,
> When I rise to worlds unknown and behold Thee on Thy throne,
> Rock of Ages, cleft for me, let me hide myself in Thee.
> —*Augustus M. Toplady, "Rock of Ages"*

> When we've been there ten thousand years, bright shining as the sun,
> We've no less days to sing God's praise than when we'd first begun.
> —*John Newton, "Amazing Grace"*

> O that with yonder sacred throng we at His feet may fall!
> We'll join the everlasting song, and crown Him Lord of all!
> —*Edward Perronet,*
> *"All Hail the Power of Jesus' Name"*

This collection highlights twenty-five hymns or gospel songs that have kept the glorious hope of heaven alive for God's people. Hymns such as these ought to be preserved for the spiritual benefit of future generations. Singing about our beliefs will reinforce our convictions and make the presence of God more real in our daily lives.

The Bible teaches that singing will be one of the prime activities of heaven, perhaps even the universal language there. For the child of God, however, eternal life is a present reality; thus, we should begin now to experience the joy of heaven.

> *That you may know that you have [present tense] eternal life.*
> —1 John 5:13

The Scriptures also remind us that we are already "seated with [Christ] in the heavenly realms" (Eph. 2:6). Learning to enjoy an intimate relationship with our Lord and responding with appropriate expressions of praise and worship can be a foretaste of the ultimate joy that awaits us. D. L. Moody, the noted nineteenth-century American evangelist, often reminded his hearers,

> A little faith will bring your soul to heaven,
> But much faith will bring heaven to your soul.

It is reported that Mr. Moody left this life in triumph, speaking these words:

> Earth is receding, heaven is opening, God is calling me!

May these timeless songs about eternity be used to heighten our awareness and anticipation of heaven's glorious hope, and to encourage us to live joyous lives of praise in preparation for joining the heavenly chorus to sing the endless "New Song."

> When the heavenly hosts shall gather
>   and the heavenly courts shall ring
> With the rapture of the ransomed,
>   and the *New Song* they shall sing,
> Though they come from every nation,
>   every kindred, every race,
> None can ever learn the music
>   'till he knows God's pard'ning grace.
>
> There will be no silent voices
>   in that ever-blessed throng;

There will be no faltering accents
  in that Hallelujah Song;
Like the sound of many waters
  shall the mighty anthem be
When the Lord's redeemed shall praise Him
  for the grace that set them free.

But 'tis here the theme is written,
  it is here we tune our tongue,
It is here the first glad notes of joy
  with stammering lips are sung;
It is here the first faint echoes
  of that chorus reach our ear.
We shall finish it in heaven,
  but our hearts begin it here.

–Annie Johnson Flint

1

After

Weeping may remain for a night,
but rejoicing comes in the morning.
—Psalm 30:5

After

N. B. VANDALL, 1896–1970

N. B. VANDALL, 1896–1970

1. Aft-er the toil and the heat of the day, Aft-er my trou-bles are past,
2. Aft-er the heart-aches and sighing shall cease, Aft-er the cold win-ter's blast,
3. Aft-er the shad-ows of evening shall fall, Aft-er my an-chor is cast,

Aft-er the sor-rows are tak-en a-way, I shall see Je-sus at last.
Aft-er the con-flict comes glo-ri-ous peace— I shall see Je-sus at last.
Aft-er I list to my Sav-ior's last call, I shall see Je-sus at last.

REFRAIN

He will be wait-ing for me— Je-sus, so kind and true; On His
for me— so kind and true;

beau-ti-ful throne, He will wel-come me home— Aft-er the day is through.

I have a Pilot in my ship
Who knows the trackless sea,
And He will guide me safely home
To His eternity.
—*Margaret Clarkson*
The Complete Speaker's Sourcebook
(©1996, Zondervan Inc., p. 193)

The anticipation of eternal glory is a comforting prospect for every child of God. As the apostle Paul reminded us, without this glorious hope "we are to be pitied more than all men" (1 Cor. 15:19).

N. B. Vandall, a veteran gospel evangelist and singer, has contributed a number of gospel songs that have been widely used by the Christian community. Another of his songs, "My Home, Sweet Home," is also included in this collection (p. 57). Like so many gospel hymns, "After" was forged out of a deeply emotional experience. Mr. Vandall recalled vividly the event in 1934 that prompted the writing of this hymn:

> One evening several years ago as I sat on the davenport reading the evening paper, I heard children's voices screaming and crying. Rushing outside, I saw our second boy Ted running toward me. He was choking with hysteria. Between sobs he gasped out the story. Paul, our younger son, had just been hit by a car out of control by its driver. It had dragged him some distance up the street. Paul was covered with blood when taken from under the car and was unable to speak.
>
> The doctor held very little hope for Paul's recovery. For one hour and fifteen minutes, I held on in earnest prayer while they cleaned and sewed up the head wounds and set the broken bones. Wearily I made my way back to my humble home. I tried to comfort my wife

when in my own heart I had no assurance. I fell on my knees and tried to pray, but all I could say was, "Oh God!"

Hardly had the words been uttered when God came. It seemed that Jesus knelt by my side. I could feel His arms around me and heard Him say, "Never mind, my child. Your home will be visited with sorrow; but in the afterward to come, these things shall not be. Your real home is in heaven where all tears will be wiped away."

Please do not think that I am a fanatic—but for the time, at least, I forgot my little boy lying at death's door. Brushing aside my tears, I made my way to the piano and rather quickly wrote the song "After."

Paul did recover, although his eyesight is still impaired. But I thank God every day for His goodness in giving him back to us. God in His wisdom, through a heartache, gave me a song that has since been a comfort to a vast number of His people.

Even as we enjoy our Lord's presence through all the experiences of this life, we await that day when we will be welcomed to our eternal heavenly home.

———————————

There the song is never ended,
There the praise will never cease;
There the sorrows and afflictions
Will be lost in tranquil peace.
Never ceasing, we shall praise our God above.
—*William Williams*

Heaven will be composed of individuals who have experienced God's presence in the midst of earthly disappointments and trials.
—*Author Unknown*

Be Still, My Soul

This is what the Sovereign LORD, the Holy One of Israel,
says: "In repentance and rest is your salvation,
in quietness and trust is your strength."
—Isaiah 30:15

Be Still, My Soul

KATHARINA VON SCHLEGEL, 1697–?
Trans. JANE L. BORTHWICK, 1813–1897

JEAN SIBELIUS, 1865–1957

"Finlandia"

1. Be still, my soul; the Lord is on thy side. Bear pa-tient-
2. Be still, my soul; thy God doth un-der-take To guide the
3. Be still, my soul; the hour is has-t'ning on When we shall

ly the cross of grief or pain. Leave to thy God to
fu-ture as He has the past. Thy hope, thy con-fi-
be for-ev-er with the Lord, When dis-ap-point-ment,

or-der and pro-vide; In ev-'ry change He faith-ful
dence let noth-ing shake; All now mys-te-rious shall be
grief, and fear are gone, Sor-row for-got, love's pur-est

will re-main. Be still, my soul; thy best, thy heav'n-ly
bright at last. Be still, my soul; the waves and wind still
joys re-stored. Be still, my soul; when change and tears are

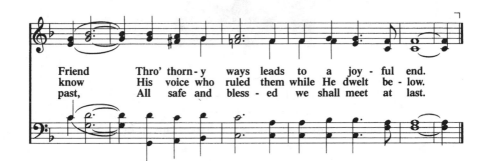

Friend   Thro' thorn - y ways leads to a joy - ful end.
know   His voice who ruled them while He dwelt be - low.
past,   All safe and bless - ed we shall meet at last.

My rest is in heaven; my rest is not here.
Then why should I murmur when trials are near?
Be hushed my sad spirit, the worst that can come
But shortens the journey and hastens me home.

The winds of affliction around me may blow
And dash my land barque as I'm sailing below;
I smile at the storm as I lean on his breast,
And soon I shall land in the haven of rest.
–Henry F. Lyte

The sovereign God who promises us a heavenly home also assures us of His presence through the "stormy ways" of this life. What encouragement this gives the child of God; we have a confidence that cannot be shaken regardless of life's circumstances. Our example is Jesus, "who for the joy set before him endured the cross, scorning its shame, and sat down at the right hand of the throne of God" (Heb. 12:2).

With its origin in the seventeenth-century Lutheran church, this fine hymn reminds us of the way the Christian life should be lived in the light of the heavenly joys that await us. The text was the product of a fervent Piestic revival in Germany, which was similar to the Puritan and Wesleyan movements in England about the same time.

Katharina von Schlege was the outstanding woman of this revival movement. Little is known of her except that she was a Lutheran and, possibly, the canoness of an evangelical women's seminary in Germany. She did contribute a number of lyrics to a collection of spiritual songs published in 1752. Though Katharina wrote other verses for this particular hymn, most hymnals use just the three stanzas included here. Approximately one hundred years after it was written, the German text was translated into English by Jane Borthwick, a Scottish woman who devoted her life to a ministry of missionary and social work.

Miss Borthwick was a member of the Free Church of Scotland and a zealous supporter of home and foreign missions.

The music was composed by Jean Sibelius, Finland's best-known composer. His music is generally characterized by a strong nationalistic fervor. This hymn tune is an arrangement of one movement of "Finlandia," a tone poem written in 1899 to convey the majestic natural beauty of the composer's native land.

Do not long merely for the heavenly rest. Rather, fix your focus on Him who is and will be our eternal rest. Reflect often on the truths of this hymn:

- "The Lord is on thy side"
- "In every change He faithful will remain"
- "All now mysterious shall be bright at last"
- "All safe and blessed we shall meet at last"

> *Do not let your hearts be troubled. Trust in God; trust also in me.*
> —John 14:1

The highest joy that can be known
by those who heav'nward wend—
It is the Word of Life to own,
and God to have as friend.
—Andrew Frykman

Christ for me is waiting, watching,
Waiting 'till I come.
Long the blessed Guide has led me
By the desert road;
Now I see the golden towers,
City of my God.
—Paul Gerhardt

Lord, grant to me a quiet mind, that trusting Thee . . . for Thou art kind . . . I may go on without a fear, for Thou, my Lord, art always near.
—Author Unknown

3

Beyond the Sunset

Now we see but a poor reflection;
then we shall see face to face. Now I know in part;
then I shall know fully, even as I am fully known.
—1 Corinthians 13:12

Beyond the Sunset

VIRGIL P. BROCK, 1887–1978   BLANCHE KERR BROCK, 1888–1958

1. Be - yond the sun - set, O bliss-ful morn - ing, When with our Sav - ior heav'n is be - gun; Earth's toil-ing end - ed, O glo - rious dawn - ing— Be - yond the sun - set when day is done.

2. Be - yond the sun - set no clouds will gath - er, No storms will threat-en, no fears an - noy; O day of glad -ness, O day un - end - ing— Be - yond the sun - set, e - ter - nal joy!

3. Be - yond the sun - set a hand will guide me To God the Fa - ther, whom I a - dore; His glo - rious pres -ence, His words of wel - come, Will be my por - tion on that fair shore.

4. Be - yond the sun - set, O glad re - un - ion With our dear loved ones who've gone be - fore; In that fair home-land we'll know no part - ing— Be - yond the sun - set for - ev - er - more!

I shall see the King in his beauty,
In the land that is far away,
When the shadows at length have lifted,
And the darkness has turned to day.

I shall see him, I shall be like him,
By one glance of his face transformed;
And this body of sin and darkness
To the image of Christ conformed.
                                        –A. J. Gordon

"*I*'ve just never seen a more beautiful sunset."

This remark by Horace Burr, a blind cousin, prompted song writer Virgil Brock to pen the lines of "Beyond the Sunset." It has become one of the most widely used songs about the hereafter in the entire field of gospel hymnody.

Virgil P. Brock wrote more than five hundred gospel songs, most of which were in collaboration with his first wife, Blanche. Virgil often joked, "After Blanche had notated the melody of my song and supplied the necessary harmony, I couldn't even read the notes." After Blanche's death in 1958, a large monument was erected in the Brock's hometown at the Warsaw-Winona Lake Cemetery, Indiana, with the words and music of "Beyond the Sunset" engraved in stone as a tribute to the ministry of this godly couple. Virgil left the following account regarding the writing of this all-time favorite song:

> The song was born during a conversation at the dinner table one evening in 1936. We had been watching a very unusual sunset at Winona Lake, Indiana, with a blind guest, my cousin Horace Burr, and his wife Grace. A large area of the water appeared ablaze with the glory of God, yet there were threatening storm clouds gathering overhead.

Our blind guest excitedly remarked: "I've just never seen a more beautiful sunset."

I responded, "People are always amazed when you talk about seeing, Horace."

"I can see," he replied. "I see through other people's eyes, and I think I can see more clearly because I see beyond the sunset."

The phrase "beyond the sunset" and the inflection of his voice struck me so forcibly. . . . I began singing the first few measures.

"That's beautiful," his wife interrupted. "Virgil, please go to the piano and sing that phrase again."

We went to the piano and soon completed the first verse. Then our guests urged, "Now you should try a verse about the storm clouds."

And the words for this verse came quickly as well. Recalling how for so many years our guests had walked hand in hand together due to his blindness, the third verse was soon added. Before the evening meal was finished, all four stanzas had been written, and we sang the entire song together.

One of Mr. Brock's delights was leading a congregation in vibrant singing. His exuberant spirit soon infected any audience. Improvising choruses for a service or composing a custom song for a special occasion became hallmark characteristics of Virgil Brock's effective ministry, which lasted to the very end of his ninety-one years.

This glorious hope revives our courage for the way,
When each in expectation lives and longs to see the day
When from sorrow, toil, pain, and sin, we shall be free,
And perfect love and joy shall reign throughout all eternity.
—John Fawcett

An eternal hope is the oxygen of the soul.
—Author Unknown

4

Face to Face

Dear friends, now we are children of God,
and what we will be has not yet been made known.
But we know that when he appears, we shall be like him,
for we shall see him as he is.

—1 John 3:2

Face to Face

CARRIE E. BRECK, 1855–1934

GRANT C. TULLAR, 1869–1950

1. Face to face with Christ, my Sav - ior, Face to face–what will it be
2. On - ly faint - ly now I see Him, With the dark-ling veil be - tween;
3. What re - joic - ing in His pres-ence, When are ban-ished grief or pain,
4. Face to face– O bliss-ful mo-ment! Face to face- to see and know;

When with rap - ture I be-hold Him, Je - sus Christ who died for me?
But a bless-ed day is com - ing, When His glo - ry shall be seen.
When the crook-ed ways are straight-ened And the dark things shall be plain.
Face to face with my Re - deem - er, Je - sus Christ who loves me so!

Refrain

Face to face I shall be-hold Him, Far be-yond the star-ry sky;

Face to face, in all His glo - ry, I shall see Him by and by!

Face to face—and that forever;
Face to face, where naught can sever;
I shall see Him in His beauty, face to face;
I have caught faint glimpses here,
Seen through many a falling tear,
But—what glory when I see Him face to face!
—*Annie Johnson Flint*

*O*ur first glimpse of Christ in his exalted state will be heaven's most thrilling moment. The psalmist expressed it well:

And I—in righteousness I will see your face;
when I awake, I will be satisfied with seeing your likeness.
—Psalm 17:15

Although by her own admission she had no sense of pitch and could not carry a tune, the author of this text had a keen sense of rhythm and a great love for music. Mrs. Carrie E. Breck, a deeply committed Christian and a lifelong member of the Presbyterian church, left the following account of her busy life as a wife, mother, and writer: "I penciled verses under all conditions; over a mending basket, with a baby on my arm, and sometimes even when sweeping or washing dishes—my mind moved in poetic meter." She wrote more than two thousand poems, a number of which have become hymn texts.

Mrs. Breck occasionally sent one of her poems to the Rev. Grant Tullar, a Methodist evangelist and gospel musician, with the request that he would set the words to suitable music. On one amazing occasion, Rev. Tullar had just completed the words and music for a song to be used at an evangelistic service. The more he reflected on his own text, however, the more it did not fully please him. Mrs. Breck's text arrived and was a perfect fit for the music he had composed. Since its publication in 1899, the hymn has been widely used by Christians in their anticipation of heaven's crowning joy.

In *Unfamiliar Stories of Familiar Hymns* by William Hart, a story is told of the Rev. and Mrs. Porteous, missionaries with the former China Inland Mission Board, and their use of this hymn while expecting death from a band of Chinese terrorists. After being led to a lonely spot on a hill, the couple heard their captors say, "This is the place!" When the executioner took his long knife from his shoulder, the courageous missionaries began to sing:

> Face to face with Christ my Savior,
> Face to face—what will it be?
> When with rapture I behold Him,
> Jesus Christ who died for me!

To the couple's surprise, no order was given. The executioner shouldered his ax-like knife, and Mr. and Mrs. Porteous were released and permitted to return to their headquarters in Shanghai. They often told this story of singing their faith in the moment when they expected death, in anticipation of seeing their Savior "face to face."

Anticipate the moment of beholding your Savior face to face—to fully "see and know," when the "crooked ways are straightened, and the dark things shall be plain."

> I shall not have lived until I have seen God;
> and when I have seen Him, I shall never die!
> *—John Donne*

5

Fade, Fade, Each Earthly Joy

I consider that our present sufferings are not worth comparing with the glory that will be revealed in us.
—Romans 8:18

Fade, Fade, Each Earthly Joy

JANE C. BONAR, 1821–1884

THEODORE E. PERKINS, 1831–1912

"Lundie"

1. Fade, fade, each earth - ly joy; Je - sus is mine. Break ev - ery
2. Tempt not my soul a - way; Je - sus is mine. Here would I
3. Fare - well, ye dreams of night; Je - sus is mine. Lost in this
4. Fare - well, mor - tal - i - ty; Je - sus is mine. Wel - come, e -

ten - der tie; Je - sus is mine. Dark is the wil - der - ness,
ev - er stay; Je - sus is mine. Per - ish - ing things of clay,
dawn - ing bright, Je - sus is mine. All that my soul has tried
ter - ni - ty; Je - sus is mine. Wel - come, O loved and blest,

Earth has no rest-ing-place, Je - sus a - lone can bless; Je - sus is mine.
Born but for one brief day, Pass from my heart a - way; Je - sus is mine.
Left but a dis-mal void; Je - sus has sat - is - fied; Je - sus is mine.
Wel-come sweet scenes of rest, Wel-come, my Sav-iour's breast; Je - sus is mine.

The pleasures of earth I have seen fade away;
They bloom for a season, but soon they decay;
But pleasures more lasting in Jesus are given,
Salvation on earth and a mansion in heaven.
—*Author Unknown*

*T*he more we reflect about heaven, the more the attractions of earth begin to fade. A mark of a mature Christian faith is when we can affirm with this hymn writer, "Farewell, mortality; welcome, eternity; Jesus is mine."

Focusing our thoughts on the glories of heaven, however, should not be an excuse for neglecting present realities. There's an old saying about being so heavenly minded that we are of no earthly good. The expectation of heaven should, rather, be an incentive to live this life as a worthy representative for our Lord, so that we will hear His "well done . . . enter thou into the joy of thy lord" (Matt. 25:21 KJV).

He liveth long who liveth well! All other life is vain;
He liveth longest who can tell of living most for heavenly gain.
—*Horatius Bonar*

Living solely for heavenly gain, however, is certainly not the case with most of us. We become so involved with the trivialities of life and the pursuit of happiness that we give little thought to eternity. A foretaste of heaven's joys is gained by filling our minds with thoughts that are true, noble, pure, lovely, admirable, and praiseworthy (Phil. 4:8), and by sensing an awareness of Christ's daily presence.

All that my soul has tried left but a dismal void;
Jesus has satisfied—Jesus is mine.

The author of this devotional text, Jane C. Bonar, was the wife of Dr. Horatius Bonar, generally regarded as one of Scotland's most gifted and powerful evangelical ministers and hymn writers. He wrote approximately six hundred hymns, one hundred of which are still in use. Jane, too, was a gifted writer and a leader in the Scottish Free Church Movement.

"Fade, Fade, Each Earthly Joy" first appeared in her husband's collection, *Songs in the Wilderness,* published in 1844. Of Mrs. Bonar's many writings, this is the one hymn for which she is still remembered. Her thoughts about earthly joys compared with the glories of eternity should reflect the sentiments of every Christian.

Lay hold on eternal life. Get hold of it now. It is a thing of the future, and it is a thing of the present; and even your part of it which is future can be, by faith, so realized and grasped as to be actually enjoyed while you are here.

—Charles H. Spurgeon

The love of heaven makes us heavenly.

—William Shakespeare

Fill every part of me with praise;
Let all my being speak
Of Thee and of Thy love, O Lord,
Poor though I be and weak.

So shalt Thou, Lord, from me, e'en me,
Receive the glory due;
And so shall I begin on earth
The song forever new.

—Horatius Bonar

Aim at heaven and you get earth thrown in. Aim at earth and you get neither.

—C. S. Lewis

6

God's Tomorrow

And God shall wipe away all tears from their eyes;
and there shall be no more death, neither sorrow, nor crying,
neither shall there be any more pain: for the former things
are passed away.

—Revelation 21:4 KJV

God's Tomorrow

A. H. ACKLEY, 1887–1960

A. H. ACKLEY, 1887–1960

1. God's tomorrow is a day of glad-ness, And its joys shall nev-er fade:
2. God's tomorrow is a day of greet-ing: We shall see the Savior's face;
3. God's tomorrow is a day of glo - ry: We shall wear the crown of life;

No more weeping, no more sense of sad-ness, No more foes to make a-fraid.
And our longing hearts a-wait the meeting In that ho - ly, hap-py place.
Sing thro' countless years love's old, old story, Free for - ev - er from all strife.

REFRAIN

God's to - mor - row, God's to - mor - row, Ev-'ry cloud will pass a-way

At the dawning of that day; God's to-mor - row, No more sor - row,

For I know that God's to - mor - row Will be brighter than to - day!

Oh, the sheer joy of it!
Ever to be
Living in glory,
Living with Thee;
Lord of tomorrow,
Lover of me!
            —R. S. Cushman

The secret of victorious Christian living is the ability to view today's cares and concerns in the light of "God's Tomorrow." The glorious hope of heaven! What cheer this prospect brings to hearts that often are burdened with discouragement and despair. What a future there is for the believer in Christ—living and reigning with Him forever and ever. Only in the gospel of the Bible do hurting people find such comfort and hope. Knowing with conviction that "God's tomorrow will be brighter than today" provides fortitude for facing circumstances that otherwise would weigh us down, especially when often our only response is *Why?* In heaven we will fully understand all of the unanswered questions of our earthly journey (1 Cor. 13:12).

The Ackley brothers—Alfred H. and Benton D.—were prominent names in the development of gospel hymnody. B. D. Ackley ministered for eight years as the pianist/secretary for the Billy Sunday-Homer Rodeheaver evangelistic team. Both Ackley brothers were associated with the Rodeheaver Publishing Company in the writing and compiling of numerous music collections. B. D. Ackley is the composer of "Sunrise," also in this book (p. 95).

A. H. Ackley, author and composer of "God's Tomorrow," was an ordained Presbyterian minister as well as an accomplished concert cellist. Even while pastoring churches in Pennsylvania and California, he maintained a keen interest in writing gospel songs, approximately one thousand before his death in 1960. Another of his well-known songs is "He Lives." In recognition of his many contributions to sacred music, Alfred Ackley was awarded an honorary Doctor of Sacred Music degree by John Brown University.

If we are wholeheartedly devoted to Christ, we can't help being heavenly minded. And the love of heaven will produce a Christlikeness in our lives today while we patiently await "God's Tomorrow."

Not now but in the coming years,
It will be in the better land,
We'll read the meaning of our tears,
And there sometime we'll understand.

We'll catch the broken threads again,
And finish what we here began;
Heaven will its mysteries explain;
Ah, then, ah, then, we'll understand.
                                    —Maxwell Cornelius

Make me ever ready to come before you with
    clean hands and a straight eye,
So as life fades away as a fading sunset,
My spirit may come to you without shame.
                                    —An Indian Prayer

Faith is to believe what we do not see, and the
reward of faith is to see what we believe.
                                    —St. Augustine

7

He the Pearly Gates Will Open

Therefore, my brothers, be all the more eager to make your calling and election sure. For if you do these things, you will never fall, and you will receive a rich welcome into the eternal kingdom of our Lord and Savior Jesus Christ.

—2 Peter 1:10–11

He the Pearly Gates Will Open

FREDRICK A. BLOM, 1867–1927
Trans. NATHANIEL CARLSON, 1879–1957

ELSIE AHLWEN, 1905–?

1. Love di - vine, so great and won - drous, Deep and might - y, pure, sub - lime;
2. Like a dove when hunt - ed, fright-ened, As a wound-ed fawn was I;
3. Love di - vine, so great and won - drous! All my sins He then for - gave.
4. In life's e - ven-tide, at twi - light, At His door I'll knock and wait;

Com - ing from the heart of Je - sus, Just the same thro' tests of time!
Bro - ken-heart - ed, yet He healed me. He will heed the sin - ner's cry.
I will sing His praise for - ev - er, For His blood, His pow'r to save.
By the pre - cious love of Je - sus, I shall en - ter heav-en's gate.

Refrain

He the pearl - y gates will o - pen, So that I may en - ter in;

For He pur-chased my re - demp - tion, And for-gave me all my sin.

It had a great, high wall with twelve gates, and with twelve
angels at the gates. . . . The twelve gates were twelve pearls, each
gate made of a single pearl.

—Revelation 21:12, 21

To that Jerusalem above with singing I repair;
While in the flesh my hope and love, my heart and soul are there.
There my exalted Savior stands, my merciful High Priest,
And still extends his wounded hands to take me to his breast.

—Charles Wesley

*W*e do not reach the gates of the New Jerusalem as described in the final book of the Bible by our own unaided efforts. Heaven is not an achievement but a reception.

When I stand before the throne,
Dressed in beauty not my own,
When I see thee as thou art,
Love thee with unsinning heart,
Then, Lord, shall I fully know,
Not 'till then how much I owe.

—R. Murray McCheyne

The twelve gates mentioned in Scripture also signify that access to heaven is not limited to any one people or geographical location. There will be redeemed representatives from every tribe, language, people, and nation (Rev. 5:9).

Out of the repentant heart of a backslidden Swedish pastor came this deeply emotional and vividly worded text. After serving with the Salvation Army and pastoring several churches, Fredrick A. Blom somehow fell into deep sin and was imprisoned in New York state. It is thought that while in prison he wrote this text as a testimony of his repentance and spiritual restoration. His second stanza is especially personal and descriptive:

Like a dove when hunted, frightened, As a wounded fawn was I;
Brokenhearted, yet He healed me. He will heed the sinner's cry.

Following his release from prison, Fredrick Blom eventually returned to Sweden, where he faithfully pastored churches until his home going in 1927.

The composer, Elsie R. Ahlwen, was also born in Sweden and came to the United States as a young woman. After her studies at the Moody Bible Institute, she became a full-time evangelist in reaching the Swedish immigrant population in the Chicago area. *"Han skall oppna parleporten"* ("He the Pearly Gates Will Open") became the popular theme song of her ministry.

How good it is to know that when the Lord calls us home, the pearly gates will open—not due to our worthiness but because "He purchased my redemption and forgave me all my sin."

Rejoice in the promises of Scripture that assure us of the rich welcome awaiting believers in Christ when we enter heaven's gates.

> My heart is glad, I'm saved by grace;
>   to Christ my life I give;
> And He's prepared for me a place,
>   where I with Him shall live.
>
> In heaven's land, heav'ns glory land,
>   we'll live eternally,
> Our home prepared by Christ's dear hand,
>   and there His face we'll see.
>
> In heav'n with Christ, we'll sing with joy,
>   no tears our eyes will dim;
> And sin shall ne'er our hope destroy,
>   when we're at home with him.
>
> —N. Frykman
> Trans. by Ethel Larson Palm

Salvation is by atonement, not attainment; by believing, not achieving.
—*Author Unknown*

8

Holy, Holy Is What the Angels Sing

Then I looked and heard the voice of many angels,
numbering thousands upon thousands, and ten thousand
times ten thousand. . . . In a loud voice they sang:
"Worthy is the Lamb, who was slain,
to receive power and wealth and wisdom and strength
and honor and glory and praise!"

—Revelation 5:11–12

Holy, Holy Is What the Angels Sing

JOHNSON OATMAN, JR., 1856–1922   JOHN R. SWENEY, 1837–1899

1. There is sing-ing up in heav-en such as we have nev-er known,
2. But I hear an-oth-er an-them, blending voi-ces clear and strong,
3. Then the an-gels stand and lis-ten, for they can-not join that song,
4. So, although I'm not an an-gel, yet I know that o-ver there

Where the an-gels sing the prai-ses of the Lamb up-on the throne;
"Un-to Him who hath redeemed us and hath bought us," is the song;
Like the sound of man-y wa-ters, by that hap-py blood-washed throng;
I will join a bless-ed cho-rus that the an-gels can-not share;

Their sweet harps are ev-er tune-ful and their voi-ces al-ways clear,
We have come thro' trib-u-la-tions to this land so fair and bright,
For they sing a-bout great tri-als, bat-tles fought and vic-t'ries won,
I will sing a-bout my Sav-iour who up-on dark Cal-va-ry

Oh, that we might be more like them while we serve the Mas-ter here.
In the foun-tain free-ly flow-ing He hath made our gar-ments white.
And they praise their great Re-deem-er who hath said to them, "Well done."
Free-ly par-doned my transgressions, died to set a sin-ner free.

CHORUS

Ho-ly, ho-ly, is what the an-gels sing, And I ex-pect to

help them make the courts of heaven ring; But when I sing redemption's sto-ry

they will fold their wings, For angels nev-er felt the joy that our sal-va-tion brings.

Hark! Ten thousand harps and voices
Sound the note of praise above;
Jesus reigns and heav'n rejoices,
Jesus reigns, the God of love.
See, He sits on yonder throne:
Jesus rules the world alone.

—*Thomas Kelly*

As God's children we often reflect about the anticipated sights of heaven—golden streets, jasper walls, crystal seas, jeweled crowns—but what about the sounds of heaven? The Bible states that heaven is filled with majestic music. A choir of angels—so vast it can not be numbered—joyously sings praise to Christ. And the thrilling truth is that we redeemed mortals will join in that heavenly chorus. The theme of heaven's inspiring music will be the worthiness of the Lamb who, in victory, secured our redemption and is alive forevermore.

The "Angel Song," as this hymn is often called, is the product of two well-known early gospel musicians, Johnson Oatman Jr. and John R. Sweney. Both of these men made significant contributions to the development of gospel hymnody. Though Mr. Oatman wrote more than five thousand hymn texts, including such songs still in use as "Count Your Blessings," "Higher Ground," and "No, Not One!" he was primarily a layman who throughout his life was a successful businessman. John Sweney was for twenty-five years a music teacher at the Pennsylvania Military Academy and was also a longtime church choir director. He composed over one thousand hymn tunes and assisted in the compilation of more than sixty collections of gospel songs, anthems, and Sunday school music.

It is said that Oatman and Sweney were one day sharing an interesting discussion about what the music of heaven would be like. The subject of angels and their role in leading the heavenly chorus especially fascinated them. Soon their thoughts were put into musical form with the completion of the "Angel Song."

The Scriptures have much to say about angels, and a biblical survey about these servants of God is an interesting study. Angels were created by God at the dawn of creation. Job 38:7 tells how the angels rejoiced when the earth was created and again when the birth of Jesus was announced to the world (Luke 2:13-14). Angels have a twofold ministry: worshiping and serving God in heaven, and serving those "who shall be heirs of salvation" (Heb. 1:14 KJV).

The Scriptures also relate that the angels rejoice in the presence of God every time one sinner repents (Luke 15:10). If the angels rejoiced at the time of our conversion, think how they will rejoice when we join forces with them in heaven's eternal choir.

I cannot tell how all the lands shall worship
When at his bidding, every storm is stilled,
Or who can say how great the jubilation
When all the hearts of men with love are filled;
But this I know, the skies will thrill with rapture,
As myriad, myriad heaven's voices sing,
And earth to heaven, and heaven to earth will answer:
"At last the Savior of the world is King!"
—*William Fullerton*

Heaven is revealed to earth as the homeland of music.
—*C. Rossetti*

Appreciate this difference: Humans in heaven are *redeemed.* Angels in heaven are created, unfallen, but *unredeemed;* they have "never felt the joy that our salvation brings."

9

How Beautiful Heaven Must Be

I saw the Holy City, the new Jerusalem, coming down out of heaven from God, prepared as a bride beautifully dressed for her husband. And I heard a loud voice from the throne saying, "Now the dwelling of God is with men, and he will live with them. They will be his people, and God himself will be with them and be their God."

—Revelation 21:2–3

How Beautiful Heaven Must Be

MRS. A. S. BRIDGEWATER, 1873–1957

A. P. BLAND, 1876–1938

1. We read of a place that's called heav-en, It's made for the pure and the free; These truths in God's word He has giv - en, How beau - ti - ful heav-en must be.
2. In heav-en, no droop-ing, nor pin-ing, No wish-ing for else-where to be, God's light is for-ev-er there shin - ing, How beau - ti - ful heav-en must be.
3. Pure wa-ters of life there are flow-ing, And all who will drink may be free; Rare je-wels of splen-dor are glow-ing, How beau - ti - ful heav-en must be.

Refrain

How beau - ti - ful heav-en must be, must be, Sweet home of the hap-py and free; Fair ha-ven of rest for the wea - ry, How beau - ti - ful heav-en must be.

Jerusalem, my happy home,
When shall I come to thee?

O happy harbor of the saints!
O sweet and pleasant soil!

In thee no sorrow may be found,
No grief, no care, no toil.

But there they live in such delight,
Such pleasure and such play,
As that to them a thousand years
Doth seem as yesterday.
—*St. Augustine*

It is always thrilling to reflect on the indescribable glory of heaven, a beauty that is beyond our wildest imagination. There we will experience the perfection of God in all its fullness. Every imperfection and frailty known in this life will be gone forever. It will be like living in the beautiful Garden of Eden before sin entered the world.

If God hath made this world so fair,
Where sin and death abound,
How beautiful, beyond compare
Will paradise be found.
—*James Montgomery*

The final two chapters of the book of Revelation provide the most complete description of the beauty that awaits us. Here we are told that the city of God will be a perfect cube with fifteen-hundred-mile proportions in height, width, and length—an indication of its immensity. There is also the mention of rare jewels, a crystal river that never runs dry, fruit trees that bear perpetual fruit, gigantic pearly gates, and streets of pure, flawless gold.

Yet this is merely a glimpse of that eternal beauty. Our mortal minds would be unable to grasp the complete picture. It would be like trying to describe the beauty of the Grand Canyon to a three-year-old child or interpreting the sounds of a Beethoven symphony to a deaf person. The main objective of the Scriptures is to acquaint us with the One who has made our entry into heaven possible. We will then have an eternity to discover just "how beautiful heaven must be."

Though little is known of Mrs. Bridgewater and A. P. Bland, author and composer of this song, we are grateful for their musical contribution, which stirs our anticipation of heaven and reminds us that our Creator God is truly a God of beauty who "has made everything beautiful in its time" (Eccl. 3:11). Our present responsibility is to worship Him not only "in spirit and in truth" (John 4:24) but also in the "beauty of holiness" (Ps. 96:9 KJV).

I'm told of a land of sheer beauty,
So great it can never be told;
A land of perennial sunshine,
A land that will never grow old.
A land of most wonderful mountains,
Its trees never wither, we're told.
Yes, heaven is wondrous in beauty,
Its glory a sight to behold.

—Anonymous

O Lord, grant that I may desire Thee, and desiring Thee, seek Thee, and seeking Thee, find Thee, and finding Thee, be satisfied with Thee forever.

—St. Augustine

10

I Know I'll See Jesus Some Day

When Christ, who is your life, appears, then you
also will appear with him in glory.
—Colossians 3:4

I Know I'll See Jesus Some Day

AVIS B. CHRISTIANSEN, 1895–1985

SCOTT LAWRENCE

1. Sweet is the hope that is thrill-ing my soul— I know I'll see
2. Though I must trav-el by faith, not by sight, I know I'll see
3. Dark-ness is gath-'ring, but hope shines with-in, I know I'll see

Je-sus some day! Then what if the dark clouds of sin o'er me roll,
Je-sus some day! No e-vil can harm me, no foe can af-fright—
Je-sus some day! What joy when He comes to wipe out ev-'ry sin;

Chorus

I know I'll see Je-sus some day! . . . I know I'll see Je-sus some
day! . . . I know I'll see Je-sus some day! . . . What a joy it will
some day! some day!

be When His face I shall see, I know I'll see Je-sus some day!

I praise him because he appointed a place
Where, some day, through faith in his wonderful grace
I know I shall see him—shall look on his face,
For he is so precious to me.

—Charles H. Gabriel

*T*he Bible speaks of three abiding essentials for the Christian life:

Faith—Hope—Love

—1 Corinthians 13:13

Faith relates to our placing complete trust in Christ's atonement as redemption paid for our eternal salvation. Faith is also necessary for trusting His divine guidance in every area of our daily lives.

Without faith it is impossible to please God.

—Hebrews 11:6

Hope is confidence in Christ's promised future. Hope is a synonym for the heavenly destiny of each believer.

Christ in you, the hope of glory.

—Colossians 1:27

Love relates to our practical relationship with other people and with God.

*Live a life of love, just as Christ loved us and gave himself up for
us as a fragrant offering and sacrifice to God.*

—Ephesians 5:2

Experiencing the ultimate joy of heaven—the privilege of seeing Jesus—involves all three of these essentials. Without exercising *faith* in Christ's sacrificial death and in His resurrection, there would be no possibility of entering heaven. Our *hope* for the promised future is a powerful motive for holy living: "to live self-controlled, upright and godly lives in this present age, while we wait for the blessed hope—the glorious appearing of our great God and Savior, Jesus Christ" (Titus 2:12-13). The *love* that we have shared with our Lord as well as with friends and loved ones in this life will be culminated and continued in heaven. *"The greatest of these is love."*

> I am living for the moment when before his feet I fall,
> And with all the host of heaven own him Lord and King of all,
> Evermore to sing the praises of the Lamb of Calvary,
> And to worship and adore him throughout all eternity.
> *—Avis B. Christiansen*

Mrs. Avis B. Christiansen is one of the important gospel hymn writers of the twentieth century. She has written hundreds of gospel hymn texts as well as several volumes of published poems. Several of her other well-known gospel songs are "Only Glory By and By," "Blessed Redeemer," and "Blessed Calvary."

Let your soul come alive with the thrill of expectancy—enjoyment of the glories of heaven and the assurance of personally seeing Jesus some day.

> When in wonder I stand with my hand in His hand, in that home with the ransomed forever, the sorrow all passed—triumphant at last—oh, what will it be to see Jesus?
> *—Fred P. Morris*

Until that thrilling day, enjoy the three abiding essentials of your Christian life. Reflect often on the difference faith, hope, and love make in daily living.

> Faith initiates our relationship with Christ,
> Hope maintains its vitality,
> Love is its supreme demonstration.
> *—Author Unknown*

11

My Home, Sweet Home

But rejoice that you participate in the sufferings of Christ, so that you may be overjoyed when his glory is revealed.

—1 Peter 4:13

My Home, Sweet Home

N. B. VANDALL, 1896–1970

N. B. VANDALL, 1896–1970

1. Walk-ing a-long life's road one day, I heard a voice so sweet-ly say, "A
2. Loved ones up-on that shore I'll meet, Casting their crowns at Je-sus' feet; I'll
3. Life's day is short— I soon shall go To be with Him who loved me so; I

place up in heav'n I am build-ing thee, A beau-ti-ful, beau-ti-ful home."
wor-ship and praise Him for-ev-er-more In my beau-ti-ful, beau-ti-ful home.
see in the dis-tance that shin-ing shore, My beau-ti-ful, beau-ti-ful home.

Home, sweet home, home, sweet home— Where I'll nev-er roam!

I see the light of that cit-y so bright— My home, sweet home.

We see but dimly through the mists and vapors,
Amid these earthly damps;
What seem to us but sad funeral tapers
May be heaven's distant lamps.
                    —Henry Wadsworth Longfellow

A view of heaven often is seen most clearly during the traumatic experiences of life. This was true for veteran evangelist and musician, N. B. Vandall, the author and composer of "My Home, Sweet Home." Mr. Vandall related this account:

> In the early spring of 1926, I returned home from a very successful campaign held in a large church. The crowds had been large and many people had found Christ as Savior. As far as I could see, the meetings had been successful, except for one thing; they had overlooked my offering. The pastor and members of the church gave me a great send-off at the train and told me that I had been a real blessing to them. They patted me on the back and said, "God bless you, the Lord will provide."
>
> Arriving home I found my wife and boys sick, which made matters no better for me. I was feeling plenty low myself—no money for rent, grocery bill, or anything else—and only a few days to spend with the family before leaving for another campaign.

Vandall's wife was also broken in spirit and deeply discouraged about being left alone with the children while he was away preaching; it was more than the evangelist could handle. He felt certain that his ministry had come to an end. Mr. Vandall remembered vividly the next few moments when he and his wife prayed together:

> We laughed and cried together, rejoicing in the sweetness of the Lord's presence. He was so near it seemed that I could reach out my

hand and touch Him. I could hear His voice speaking these words of comfort to my heart: "Son, be faithful just a few more years, and I'll give you a home you'll never have to leave, where good-byes will never come, and where heartaches cannot enter."

Brushing back the tears, I made my way to the piano. The words seemed to rush forth to meet the melody ringing in my mind. In a very short time "My Home, Sweet Home" was born.

N. B. Vandall is also the author and composer of the hymn "After," also in this book (p. 13).

Just think of stepping on shore, and finding it heaven!
Of taking hold of a hand, and finding it God's hand,
Of breathing new air, and finding it celestial air;
Of feeling invigorated, and finding it immortality,
Of passing from storm and tempest to an unbroken calm—
Of waking up in glory, and finding it home.

—Anonymous

Keep the "light of that city so bright" aglow in your soul. It makes a difference!

O think of the home over there,
    by the side of the river of light,
Where the saints, all immortal and fair,
    are robed in their garments of white.

O think of the friends over there,
    who before us the journey have trod,
Of the songs that they breathe on the air,
    in their home in the palace of God.

—D. W. C. Huntington

12

My Savior First of All

You have made known to me the path of life;
you will fill me with joy in your presence,
with eternal pleasures at your right hand.
—Psalm 16:11

My Savior First of All

FANNY J. CROSBY, 1820–1915

JOHN R. SWENEY, 1837–1899

1. When my life-work is end-ed, and I cross the swell-ing tide, When the
2. O the soul-thrill-ing rap-ture when I view His bless-ed face, And the
3. O the dear ones in glo-ry– how they beck-on me to come, And our
4. Thro' the gates to the cit-y in a robe of spot-less white, He will

bright and glo-rious morn-ing I shall see, I shall know my Re-
lus-ter of His kind-ly beam-ing eye! How my full heart will
part-ing at the riv-er I re-call! To the sweet vales of
lead me where no tears will ev-er fall. In the glad song of

deem-er when I reach the oth-er side, And His smile will be the
praise Him for the mer-cy, love, and grace That pre-pare for me a
E-den they will sing my wel-come home; But I long to meet my
a-ges I shall min-gle with de-light; But I long to meet my

Refrain

first to wel-come me.
man-sion in the sky! I shall know_____ Him; I shall know Him,
Sav-ior first of all. I shall know Him;
Sav-ior first of all.

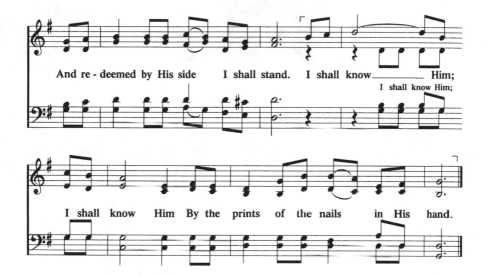

And re-deemed by His side I shall stand. I shall know———— Him;

I shall know Him;

I shall know Him By the prints of the nails in His hand.

When the praise of heaven I hear,
Loud as thunder to the ear,
Loud as many waters' voice,
Sweet as harp's melodious voice:
Then, Lord, shall I fully know,
Not 'till then how much I owe.
                    —R. Murray McCheyne

The strong and triumphant spirit of the American hymn writer Fanny Jane Crosby was an inspiration to all who knew her. Early in life Fanny showed an unusual poetic talent. At the age of eight she wrote these lines:

Oh, what a happy soul am I!
Although I cannot see,
I am resolved that in this world
Contented I will be.

How many blessings I enjoy
That other people don't;
To weep and sigh because I'm blind,
I cannot, and I won't.

Although Fanny Crosby was blind from six weeks of age because of improper medical treatment, she never exhibited bitterness or depression. Once, a well-intentioned Scottish minister remarked to her,

"I think it is a great pity that the Master, when He showered so many gifts upon you, did not give you sight."

"Do you know," responded Fanny, "if at birth I had been able to make one petition to my Creator, it would have been that I should be born blind."

"Why?" asked the surprised clergyman.

"Because when I get to heaven, the first sight that shall ever gladden my eyes will be that of my Savior!"

For Fanny Crosby, the anticipation of heaven was the joy of seeing her Savior "first of all." Although she wrote eight thousand or more gospel song texts on many different subjects, the themes of heaven and the Lord's return seem to have been her favorites. "My Savior First of All," however, portrays more strongly than any other hymn her hope of seeing the beauty of Christ's welcome—to stand by his side "in a robe of spotless white" and witness first-hand his scars of redemption.

What moving scenes Fanny Crosby created for us to ponder in these vividly worded lines first published in 1894.

———————

The only scars in heaven will be the scars of redemption borne by Christ in our behalf.

—Author Unknown

The whole creation joins as one to bless the sacred name
Of Him that sits upon the throne, and to adore the Lamb.

—Isaac Watts

But I know I shall wake in the likeness
    of Him I am longing to see;
I know that mine eyes shall behold Him,
    Who died for a sinner like me.

—Fanny J. Crosby

O great and glorious vision—
The Lamb upon His throne;
O wondrous sight for man to see
The Savior with His own,
To drink the living waters
And stand upon the shore
Where neither sorrow, sin, nor death
Shall ever enter more.

—Godfrey Thring

13

No Disappointment in Heaven

And I—in righteousness I will see your face;
when I awake, I will be satisfied with seeing your likeness.
—Psalm 17:15

No Disappointment in Heaven

F. M. LEHMAN, 1868–1953   F. M. LEHMAN, 1868–1953

1. There's no dis-ap-point-ment in heaven, No wear-i-ness, sor-row or pain;
2. We'll nev-er pay rent for our mansion, The tax-es will nev-er come due;
3. There'll nev-er be crepe on the door-knob, No fu-ner-al train in the sky;

No hearts that are bleeding and bro-ken, No song with a mi-nor re-frain;
Our gar-ments will never grow threadbare, But al-ways be fadeless and new;
No graves on the hill-sides of glo-ry, For there we shall nev-er-more die;

The clouds of our earth-ly ho-ri-zon Will nev-er ap-pear in the sky,
We'll nev-er be hun-gry nor thirst-y, Nor lan-guish in pov-er-ty there,
The old will be young there for-ev-er, Transformed in a mo-ment of time;

For all will be sun-shine and glad-ness, With nev-er a sob nor a sigh.
For all the rich boun-ties of heav-en His sanc-ti-fied chil-dren will share.
Im-mor-tal we'll stand in His like-ness, The stars and the sun to out-shine.

CHORUS.

I'm bound for that beau-ti-ful cit-y, My Lord has prepared for His own;

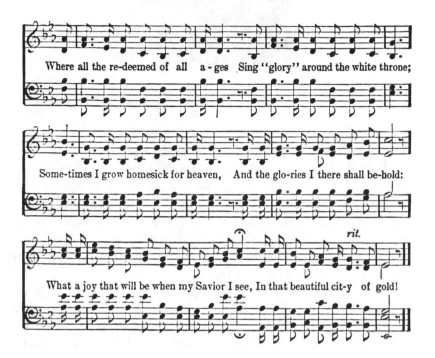

Where all the re-deemed of all a - ges Sing "glory" around the white throne;

Some-times I grow homesick for heaven, And the glo-ries I there shall be-hold:

What a joy that will be when my Savior I see, In that beautiful cit-y of gold!

Above this earthly home of ours
of chilling winds and fading flowers,
There is a home all bright and fair,
and all our hopes are centered there.
—Maggie E. Gregory

*I*t is disheartening to happily anticipate an event and then be disappointed when it occurs. This will not be true when we enter heaven. Its glories will thrill us infinitely more than we dare to imagine. In a state of wonder, awe, and excitement, we will be actively involved in serving and worshiping our Lord and reigning with Him.

The psalmist David assures us in Psalm 17:15 that heaven will be a place of complete satisfaction. He knew that he would be satisfied because he would arrive there as a righteous person, free of all taints of sin and selfishness. He would be perfect in body and soul, in heart and mind. His greatest satisfaction, however, would be the sight of his Lord's face—His very likeness.

Rev. Frederick Lehman, author and composer of this gospel hymn, enumerates examples of what heaven will be like: no disappointments; no weariness, sorrow, or pain; no rent or taxes; no hunger or thirst; no poverty; no funerals; no aging. We can readily agree with Mr. Lehman that we oftentimes "grow homesick for heaven, and the glories I there shall behold."

Nor eye has seen, nor ear has heard,
Nor sense, nor reason known,
What joys the Father has prepared
For those who love the Son.
—Isaac Watts

Frederick M. Lehman pastored several Nazarene churches throughout his early ministry in Indiana and Illinois before moving to Kansas City in 1911, where he became involved in starting the Nazarene Publishing House. Rev.

Lehman is the author of numerous poems and gospel songs, including the five popular volumes of *Songs That Are Different.* He is also the author and composer of the beloved gospel hymn "The Love of God."

Let us resolve to look away from the disappointments of this life and focus more clearly on the complete satisfaction that will be ours upon our arrival in heaven. Until then, let us set our "affection on things above, not on things on the earth" (Col. 3:2 KJV).

So shall it be at last, in that bright morning,
When the soul waketh and life's shadows flee;
Oh, in that home fairer than daylight dawning,
Shall rise the glorious thought—
    I am with Thee!
                                —Harriet Beecher Stowe

Live with the joyous anticipation of heaven's festival—a continuous celebration of the victory that Christ accomplished over death.

I do not fear tomorrow
For I have lived today;
And though my course was stormy
My Pilot knew the way.

I do not fear tomorrow!
If the sails set east or west;
On sea or safe in harbor
In Him, secure, I rest.
                                —Author Unknown

The more clearly we see the sovereignty of God, the less perplexed we are by the calamities of man.
                                —Author Unknown

14

O That Will Be Glory

He [God] will wipe every tear from their eyes. There will be
no more death or mourning or crying or pain, for the old
order of things has passed away.

—Revelation 21:4

O That Will Be Glory

CHARLES H. GABRIEL, 1856–1932   CHARLES H. GABRIEL, 1856–1932

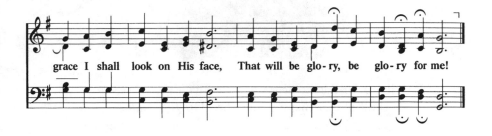

grace I shall look on His face, That will be glo-ry, be glo-ry for me!

I am living for the moment when my Savior's face I see—
O the thrill of that first meeting when His glory shines on me!
When His voice like sweetest music falls upon my waiting ear,
And my name, amid the millions, from His precious lips I hear.

—*Avis B. Christiansen*

*H*eaven will be a place of absolute joy. The same excitement, wonder, pleasures, and activities that made life rewarding and enjoyable on earth will be found in heaven. Experiences that we especially enjoy in this life are the closest we can come to understanding the delights that await us in heaven.

> *You will fill me with joy in your presence, with eternal*
> *pleasures at your right hand.*
> —Psalm 16:11

Heaven will not only be the scene of joy and pleasure but also the place where the three most dreaded experiences of this life—suffering, sorrow, and death—will be eliminated forever. One cannot reflect on these truths without being stirred with the deepest emotions and the desire to exclaim, "Glory, glory!"

Such a response was the basis for the text of "O That Will Be Glory." Author and composer Charles Gabriel was inspired by his good friend Ed Card, superintendent of the Sunshine Rescue Mission in St. Louis, Missouri. Ed was a radiant believer who bubbled over with the joy of the Lord. During a sermon or prayer he would often explode with the expression, "Glory!" Ed's smiling face earned him the nickname of "Old Glory Face." It was his custom to close his own prayers with a reference to heaven, ending with the phrase "and that will be glory for me!" It is said that Mr. Card had the joy of singing this hymn just before his home going—having the pleasure of knowing that his victorious Christian life had been its inspiration.

Charles H. Gabriel was one of the best-known and most prolific gospel songwriters of the early twentieth century. His gospel songs were used especially during the large Billy Sunday-Homer Rodeheaver evangelistic campaigns of the 1910 to 1920 decade. "O That Will Be Glory" first appeared in a publication titled *Make His Praise Glorious,* which was published in 1900. Since then it has been translated into many languages and dialects.

This song of celebration reminds us that one moment of heavenly glory will outweigh a lifetime of toil and suffering.

Heaven will be the endless portion of every man who has heaven in his soul.

—Henry Ward Beecher

When I shall see my Redeemer as He is,
    I shall be like Him.
This will be heaven indeed—to behold His
    glory without a veil,
To rejoice in His love without a cloud,
And to sing His praises without a jarring or wandering note—
    Forever!

—John Newton

"And that will be glory for me!" Allow the anticipation of heaven to radiate your countenance daily. There is a biblical precedent for this joyous response:

. . . and in his temple all cry, "Glory!"
—Psalm 29:9

Joy is the echo of God's life within us.
—Joseph Marmien

15

On Jordan's Stormy Banks

*If in this life only we have hope in Christ,
we are of all men most miserable. But now is Christ risen
from the dead, and become the firstfruits of them that
slept. . . . And as we have borne the image of the earthy,
we shall also bear the image of the heavenly.*
—1 Corinthians 15:19–20, 49 KJV

On Jordan's Stormy Banks

SAMUEL STENNETT, 1727–1795

Traditional American Melody;
arr. by RIGDON M. McINTOSH, 1836–1899
"Promised Land"

1. On Jor-dan's storm-y banks I stand, And cast a wish-ful eye
2. All o'er those wide ex-tend-ed plains Shines one e-ter-nal day;
3. No chill-ing winds nor poi-s'nous breath Can reach that health-ful shore;
4. When shall I reach that hap-py place, And be for-ev-er blest?

To Ca-naan's fair and hap-py land, Where my pos-ses-sions lie.
There God the Son for-ev-er reigns And scat-ters night a-way.
Sick-ness and sor-row, pain and death Are felt and feared no more.
When shall I see my Fa-ther's face, And in His bos-om rest?

Refrain

I am bound for the prom-ised land; I am bound for the prom-ised land.

O who will come and go with me? I am bound for the prom-ised land.

When I shall reach the more excellent glory,
And all my trials are past,
I shall be like Him, O wonderful story!
I shall be like Him at last.

—*W. A. Spencer*

*G*od's people have always been known for their anticipation. In the Old Testament, the Israelites anticipated the Promised Land, Canaan. New Testament believers anticipate the glorious hope of one day sharing eternity with their Savior and Lord.

It is enlightening to read in Joshua 3 the account of the Israelites' preparation for crossing the Jordan River en route to the Promised Land. They had to obey the instructions of Joshua, their leader, and consistently follow behind the ark of the covenant. Despite their uncertainties, they were given assurance:

> *Then you will know which way to go, since you have
> never been this way before.*
> —Joshua 3:4

We, too, will one day stand on the outmost borders of this life and view our eternal home. How important it is that we have heard the voice of Jesus, our leader, and have followed the instructions of His holy Word. And despite the uncertainties in that hour, we will be able to say with confidence,

> *You guide me with your counsel,
> and afterward you will take me into glory.*
> —Psalm 73:24

The author of this hymn, Samuel Stennett, was one of the most respected and influential preachers among the Dissenting or Non-Conformist groups of his time. He pastored a Baptist church on Little Wild Street in London, England, for an entire lifetime. Stennett was highly esteemed by all religious groups, not only for his preaching but also for his support of social reforms and religious freedom. It was said that Stennett was even a personal friend of the reigning monarch, King George III.

The tune, "Promised Land," is one of the many traditional melodies used in the United States during the early part of the nineteenth century. Its first appearance as a hymn tune can be traced back to 1835 in a hymnal called *Southern Harmony,* where it is shown with shaped notes. Later a noted southern musician named Rigdon M. McIntosh altered the tune and added the refrain. The hymn has been sung with joy by evangelical congregations since it was first published in 1895.

"O who will come and go with me?" Take time to invite others to join you on the heavenly journey.

Then let our songs abound and every tear be dry;
We're marching thru Immanuel's ground to fairer
   worlds on high.
We're marching upward to Zion, the beautiful city
   of God.
                                              —Isaac Watts

We humans make provision for this life as if it would never end; and we make provision for eternity as if it would never begin.
                                              —Anonymous

Come, let us join our joyful songs with angels round the throne; ten thousand thousand are their tongues, but all their joys are one. "Worthy the Lamb that died," they cry, "to be exalted thus; "Worthy is the Lamb," our lips reply, "for He was slain for us."
                                              —Isaac Watts

16

Over the Sunset Mountains

Surely goodness and love will follow me
  all the days of my life,
and I will dwell in the house of the LORD
  forever.

—Psalm 23:6

Over the Sunset Mountains

JOHN W. PETERSON, 1921–

JOHN W. PETERSON, 1921–

1. O - ver the sun - set moun - tains Some-day I'll soft - ly go,
2. Toil-ing will all be end - ed, Shad-ows will flee a - way;

In - to the arms of Je - sus— He who has loved me so.
Sor-row will be for - got - ten— O what a won-der-ful day!

REFRAIN

O - ver the sun - set moun - tains, Heav-en a - waits for me;

O - ver the sun - set moun - tains, Je - sus my Sav-ior I'll see.

Sunset and evening star,
And one clear call for me,
And may there be no moaning of the bar,
When I put out to sea.

For tho' from out our span of time and place
The flood may bear me far;
I hope to see my Pilot face to face
When I have crossed the bar.

—Alfred Lord Tennyson

Since World War II, the name of John W. Peterson has been associated with much fine gospel music. Over one thousand gospel songs, hymns, and choruses as well as many longer musical works such as cantatas, choral arrangements, and gospel film musicals have been written by this gifted and dedicated composer. In his book, *The Miracle Goes On* (Zondervan, 1976), John Peterson shares his conviction for writing:

> I am under obligation to communicate the gospel as much as the man in the pulpit. My song must say something to bring the lost to Christ, to challenge the Christian to dedication or service, to comfort and encourage the sorrowing and afflicted, or to be a meaningful expression of prayer and praise.

Mr. Peterson began his musical career in Kansas, where he became known as the "singing farm boy." During World War II, he served as a pilot over the China "Hump" in the Himalayas. Many of the themes for his future songs, such as "Over the Sunset Mountains," came during his flights as he viewed with awe the mighty works of nature.

Upon his return home, John enrolled in the Moody Bible Institute, where his gospel song-writing talent developed in earnest. Later he graduated from the American Conservatory of Music.

One day in 1953, while employed as a musician for Moody radio station WMBI, John sat at his piano enjoying some casual improvising. He began thinking about the glories of heaven and suddenly found himself singing and playing the chorus for "Over the Sunset Mountains." In a short time the entire song was completed and written out.

The song made an immediate impact upon the evangelical Christian community. It wasn't long before a large publishing company offered to buy John Peterson's song at an attractive price if he would simply change the phrase *Jesus, my Savior I'll see.* The idea of heaven was fine, but the reference to Jesus as Savior would be offensive to various religious groups.

John Peterson refused the publisher's offer. Instead, he wrote another song in answer to the publisher's demands. Its title was "My Song."

> I have no song to sing,
>   but that of Christ my King;
> to Him my praise I'll bring forevermore!
> His love beyond degree,
> His death that ransomed me;
>   now and eternally,
> I'll sing it o'er.
>
> *—John W. Peterson*

Lift your voice in praise to the only One who can ransom your soul and promise to guide you safely to your heavenly home.

All my theology is reduced to this narrow compass: Christ Jesus came into this world to save sinners.

—Archibald Alexander

17

Saved by Grace

Now we know that if the earthly tent we live in is destroyed,
we have a building from God, an eternal house in heaven,
not built by human hands. Meanwhile we groan,
longing to be clothed with our heavenly dwelling.

—2 Corinthians 5:1–2

Saved by Grace

FANNY J. CROSBY, 1820–1915

GEORGE C. STEBBINS, 1846–1945

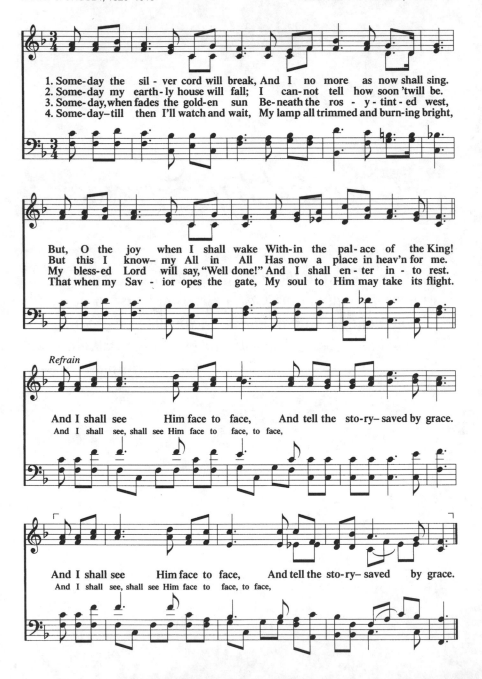

1. Some-day the sil - ver cord will break, And I no more as now shall sing.
2. Some-day my earth- ly house will fall; I can-not tell how soon 'twill be.
3. Some-day, when fades the gold-en sun Be-neath the ros - y - tint - ed west,
4. Some-day-till then I'll watch and wait, My lamp all trimmed and burn-ing bright,

But, O the joy when I shall wake With-in the pal- ace of the King!
But this I know– my All in All Has now a place in heav'n for me.
My bless-ed Lord will say, "Well done!" And I shall en - ter in - to rest.
That when my Sav - ior opes the gate, My soul to Him may take its flight.

Refrain

And I shall see Him face to face, And tell the sto-ry– saved by grace.
And I shall see, shall see Him face to face, to face,

And I shall see Him face to face, And tell the sto-ry– saved by grace.
And I shall see, shall see Him face to face, to face,

Precious, oh how precious to behold his face,
Ever to be with him and to praise his grace;
Ah, when Jesus gives his beloved sleep,
'Tis the tenderest token of his love so deep.

—Anonymous

*C*onsider the evangelical movement in the United States. It experienced a phenomenal rise during the last quarter of the nineteenth and the early years of the twentieth centuries. During that time three spiritual stalwarts stand out among the most influential: the evangelist and founder of the Moody Bible Institute, Dwight L. Moody; musician and publisher Ira D. Sankey; and hymn writer Fanny J. Crosby. In his later years, Sankey himself often remarked that the success of the Moody-Sankey evangelistic campaigns was due, more than any other human factor, to the use of Fanny Crosby's hymns.

In the period from 1870 to her death in 1915, Fanny Crosby wrote between eight and nine thousand gospel hymn texts, more than any other known writer. Her favorite motto was, "I think life is not too long, and therefore I determine that many people will read a song who would not read a sermon."

"Saved by Grace" was written by Fanny Crosby when she was seventy-one years of age. She titled her new poem "Some Day" and often referred to it as her "heart song." It became one of the most widely used hymns during the closing years of the Moody-Sankey evangelistic ministry. Fanny's text was prompted by a tract containing the final message of a pastor friend who had recently died. One statement especially moved the blind poet: "If each of us is faithful to the grace which is given us by Christ, that same grace which teaches us how to live will also teach us how to die."

"Saved by Grace" became one of the personal favorites of both Moody and Sankey during the latter period of their ministry, and they used the song at nearly every service. A recurring sight whenever the song was sung at one of these meetings was "old Moody" sitting on the platform with a far-off look in his eyes and tears running down his ruddy, whiskered cheeks. Mr. Moody loved to hear a large audience sing the hymn, especially if it could be divided between the choir and the audience. The choir would sing the phrase "and I shall see Him face to face," and the audience would respond with "and tell the story saved by grace."

Then on the morning of August 13, 1908, as Ira Sankey drifted off into a coma, it is reported that he was singing these lines:

> Some day the silver cord will break,
> And I no more as now shall sing,
> But oh the joy when I shall wake
> Within the palace of the King!

By nightfall of that day, Ira D. Sankey experienced the truth of Fanny Crosby's "heart song," the last he ever sang on earth but perhaps the one that was still on his lips as he entered heaven's portals.

If Christ is the central object of our future hope, it is because He is now the central object of our saving faith.

—*Author Unknown*

O Christ, thou King of Glory, I soon shall dwell with Thee!
I soon shall sing the praises of Thy great love to me!
Meanwhile my soul would enter e'en now before Thy throne,
That all my love might center on Thee and Thee alone.

—*Charite L. Bancroft*

To myself I will show a heart of steel,
To my fellowman a heart of love,
To my God a heart of flame.

—*St. Augustine*

18

Some Bright Morning

But your dead will live;
   their bodies will rise.
You who dwell in the dust,
   wake up and shout for joy.
Your dew is like the dew of the morning;
   the earth will give birth to her dead.
                              —Isaiah 26:19

Some Bright Morning

CHARLOTTE G. HOMER, 1856–1932

CHARLES H. GABRIEL, 1856–1932

1. Be not a-wea-ry, for la-bor will cease Some glad morn-ing;
2. Wea-ri-some bur-dens will all be laid down, Some glad morn-ing;
3. La-bor well done shall re-ceive its re-ward, Some glad morn-ing;
4. O what a time of re-joic-ing will come, Some glad morn-ing;
5. There with the loved ones who've gone on be-fore, Some glad morn-ing;

Tur-moil will change in-to in-fi-nite peace, Some bright morn-ing.
Then shall our cross be exchanged for a crown, Some bright morn-ing.
Thou who art faith-ful shall be with the Lord, Some bright morn-ing.
When all the ransomed are gathered at home, Some bright morn-ing.
We shall sing praise to the Lamb ev-er-more, Some bright morn-ing.

CHORUS

Some bright morning, Some glad morn-ing, When the sun is shin-ing in th' e-ter-nal sky; .... Some bright morn-ing, Some glad morn-ing .. We shall see the Lord of Har-vest, By and by.

We shall come with joy and gladness,
    We shall gather 'round the throne;
Face to face with those that love us,
    We shall know as we are known.
And the song of our redemption
    shall resound through endless day
When the shadows have departed
    and the mists have rolled away.
                    —Author Unknown

One of the many delights that will break upon our view when we enter heaven will be its brightness. It will be an entirely new kind of light with never any trace of darkness—"the Lamb is its lamp" (Rev. 21:23).

"Some Bright Morning" is also a reminder that rewards and crowns will be given in heaven. Christians' rewards will be based upon using, while on earth, the opportunities to minister with their God-given abilities. The Scriptures also teach that various crowns will be distributed to God's children:

- the crown of life (Rev. 2:10)
- the crown of righteousness (2 Tim. 4:8)
- the crown of glory (1 Thess. 2:19)
- the incorruptible crown (1 Cor. 9:25-27 KJV)

Another important presentation will be heaven's inhabitants receiving their new names. Revelation 2:17 states that we will be given a name that will reflect our heavenly identity. Though these rewards will vary according to our individual merits, there will be no discontent or envy in heaven. Everyone will be fully satisfied with God's justice and standards of distribution.

This song of encouragement also reminds us of the happy reunion with loved ones who have preceded us. Together we'll enjoy the fellowship of singing "praise to the Lamb evermore."

In our holy thrill of transport
They will be the first to share,
First to bid us joyous welcome—
We shall know each other there.
                              —Fanny J. Crosby

The author and composer of this gospel hymn, Charles Hutchinson Gabriel, is generally considered the most influential gospel songwriter of 1910 to 1920—the decade of the Billy Sunday-Homer Rodeheaver evangelistic crusades. It is estimated that Gabriel was involved in the writing of more than eight thousand gospel songs. For many of his songs, he wrote both the text and the music. Often, however, Gabriel attributed his texts to his pseudonym, "Charlotte G. Homer," as he did in this song.

Who are these like stars appearing,
    These before God's throne who stand?
Each a golden crown is wearing;
    Who are all this glorious band?
Alleluia! hark, they sing,
Praising loud their heavenly King.
                    —Heinrich Theobald Schenk

When life seems the darkest, anticipate the "bright morning" that awaits you. In the meantime, be concerned about storing "up for yourselves treasures in heaven. . . . For where your treasure is, there your heart will be also" (Matt. 6:20-21).

God shall wipe away all tears,
There's no death, no pain, nor tears;
And they count not time by years,
For there is no night there.
                    —John R. Clements

19

Sunrise

So will it be with the resurrection of the dead.
The body that is sown is perishable, it is raised imperishable;
it is sown in dishonor, it is raised in glory; it is sown in
weakness, it is raised in power; it is sown a natural body,
it is raised a spiritual body.

—1 Corinthians 15:42–44

Sunrise

W. C. POOLE, 1875–1949

B. D. ACKLEY, 1872–1958

1. When I shall come to the end of my way, When I shall rest at the
2. When in His beau-ty I see the great King, Join with the ran-somed His
3. When life is o - ver and day-light is passed, In heav-en's har-bor my

close of life's day, When "Wel-come home" I shall hear Je - sus say, O
prais - es to sing, When I shall join them my trib - utes to bring, O
an - chor is cast, When I see Je - sus my Sav - ior at last, O

that will be sun-rise for me. . . . .

CHORUS

Sun-rise to-mor-row, sun-rise to-mor-row, Sun-rise in glo-ry is wait-ing for me; Sun-rise to-mor-row, sun-rise to-mor-row, Sun-rise with Je - sus for e - ter - ni - ty.

We go to the grave of a friend saying,
  "A man is dead";
But angels throng about him singing,
  "A man is born."
—Henry Ward Beecher

*O*ne of the loveliest sights in all of nature is the rising sun, glowing on a distant horizon. There is something almost breathtaking about viewing the dawn of a bright new day after experiencing the blackness of nighttime.

A beautiful sunrise is a moving reminder of the resurrection of our redeemed souls. Death is not the end but the beginning of life—the sunrise of an unending day. Our worn and tired bodies will be exchanged for glorified bodies without the loss of our personal identities.

Changed from glory into glory
'Till in heav'n we take our place,
'Till we cast our crowns before Thee,
Lost in wonder, love and praise!
—Charles Wesley

Though our knowledge about what lies on the other side of the grave is sketchy, we need not fear—our Lord will be waiting to welcome us home.

O death, where is thy sting? O grave, where is thy victory? . . .
But thanks be to God, which giveth us the victory through
our Lord Jesus Christ.
—1 Corinthians 15:55, 57 KJV

Whether we are caught up to meet the Lord in the air upon His return or whether we walk the valley of the shadow of death, the future for believers is the same—"sunrise with Jesus for eternity."

The author of the "Sunrise" text, William C. Poole, was an ordained Methodist minister who served various pastorates in Maryland for thirty-five years. Rev. Poole is also the author of the well-known gospel hymn "Just When I Need Him Most."

The composer of "Sunrise," Bentley D. Ackley, was a productive gospel musician. He traveled with the Billy Sunday-Homer Rodeheaver evangelistic team for eight years while serving as its pianist/secretary and supplying new songs for the crusades. Later, as editor of the Rodeheaver Music Company, he was the composer of more than three thousand hymn tunes and the compiler of numerous collections.

Even as the beggar Lazarus was carried by the angels to Abraham's side (Luke 16:2), the Christian will be escorted by angels into the presence of Christ. It will be a glorious journey, never one to be feared.

> My Father's home on high,
>   Home of my soul how near
> At times to faith's foreseeing eye
>   Thy golden gates appear.
>
> Knowing as I am known,
>   How I shall love that word,
> And oft repeat before the throne,
>   "Forever with the Lord!"
>   *—James Montgomery*

That day which you fear as being the end of all things is the birthday of your eternity.

—Seneca

20

Sweet By-and-By

Praise be to the God and Father of our Lord Jesus Christ!
In his great mercy he has given us new birth into a living
hope through the resurrection of Jesus Christ from the dead,
and into an inheritance that can never perish,
spoil or fade—kept in heaven for you.

—1 Peter 1:3–4

Sweet By-and-By

SANFORD F. BENNETT, 1836–1898   JOSEPH P. WEBSTER, 1819–1874

Beyond this vale of tears,
There is a life above,
Unmeasured by the flight of years,
And all that life is love.
                              —James Montgomery

*T*his simply stated gospel song has been a source of much comfort to grieving Christians since it was first published in 1868. It has been especially useful as a funeral hymn, encouraging those who are mourning the loss of a loved one. For the believer in Christ the message is that we shall meet again "on that beautiful shore." What comfort this gives to grieving hearts.

> *Blessed are the dead which die in the Lord . . . that they may rest*
> *from their labours; and their works do follow them.*
>   —Revelation 14:13 KJV

The author of this text, Sanford Bennett, told an amusing story about the origin of this hymn:

> As the proprietor of a local drugstore in Elkhorn, Wisconsin, I often would visit with my many friends who dropped in to see me. One day the town musician, Joseph Webster, stopped by with his violin under his arm. Mr. Webster, like many musicians, was of an exceedingly sensitive nature and was subject to periods of depression during which he looked upon the dark side of everything in life. I had learned his peculiarities so well that on meeting him, I could tell at a glance if he was melancholy, and I had found that I could usually rouse him by giving him a new song to work on. That day he walked through the store, turned his back on me, and never spoke.

Turning to him, I said, "Webster, what is the matter now?" "It's no matter," he replied, "it will be all right by and by!" The idea of the hymn came to me like a flash of sunlight, and I replied, "The sweet by and by! Why would that not make a good hymn?" "Maybe it would," said Webster indifferently.

Turning to my desk I penned the words of the hymn as fast as I could write. I handed the words to Webster. As he read, his eyes kindled, and stepping to the desk he began writing the notes. Taking his violin, he played the melody and then jotted down the notes of the chorus. It was not over thirty minutes from the time I took my pen to write the words before Webster and I were singing the hymn together.

Before his death at the age of fifty-six, Joseph Webster was recognized as a noted musician and the composer of more than one thousand compositions. Today visitors to Elkhorn, Wisconsin, may visit the nineteenth-century Webster home and view the violin that was first used to play the melody of this comforting gospel hymn.

When our work here is done and the life crown is won
    and our troubles and trials are o'er,
All our sorrows will end and our voices will blend
    with the loved ones who've gone on before.
                                        —James C. Moore

Earth has no sorrow that heaven cannot heal.
                                        —Thomas Moore

God comforts us in our times of need in order that we in turn might learn to comfort others—"[to] provide for those who grieve . . . a garment of praise instead of a spirit of despair" (Isa. 61:3).

21

The Sands of Time Are Sinking

Whom have I in heaven but you?
   And being with you, I desire nothing on earth.
My flesh and my heart may fail,
   but God is the strength of my heart
and my portion forever.
                            —Psalm 73:25–26

The Sands of Time Are Sinking

ANNE ROSS COUSIN, 1824–1906

CHRÉTIEN URHAN, 1790–1845
Arr. by EDWARD F. RIMBAULT, 1816–1876

"Rutherford"

1. The sands of time are sink-ing, The dawn of heav-en breaks;
2. O Christ, He is the foun-tain, The deep, sweet well of love!
3. O I am my Be-lov-ed's, And my Be-lov-ed's mine!
4. The Bride eyes not her gar-ment But her dear Bride-groom's face;

The sum-mer morn I've sighed for— The fair, sweet morn a - wakes:
The streams on earth I've tast-ed More deep I'll drink a - bove:
He brings a poor vile sin-ner In-to His "house of wine."
I will not gaze at glo - ry But on my King of grace.

Dark, dark hath been the mid-night, But day-spring is at hand,
There to an o-cean ful-ness His mer-cy doth ex-pand,
I stand up-on His mer-it— I know no oth-er stand,
Not at the crown He giv-eth But on His pierc-ed hand:

And glo - ry, glo - ry dwell - eth In Im-man-uel's land.
And glo - ry, glo - ry dwell - eth In Im-man-uel's land.
Not e'en where glo - ry dwell - eth In Im-man-uel's land.
The Lamb is all the glo - ry Of Im-man-uel's land.

Once heaven seemed a far off place,
'Till Jesus showed His smiling face;
Now it's begun within my soul,
'Twill last while endless ages roll.
                                    —*C. F. Butler*

*W*e desire to dwell in heaven. But not merely to enjoy the promised sights or to hear the glorious sounds of the heavenly chorus. Rather, we desire to be with the lover of our soul and to live eternally with Him. The goal of heaven, then, is Christ Himself—not joy, nor peace, nor rest—Himself, our "King of Grace."

The Lamb is all the glory of Immanuel's land.
                                    —*A. R. Cousin*

This stirring text was written by Anne Ross Cousin approximately two hundred years after the initial events that prompted its writing. Mrs. Cousin was a gifted nineteenth-century English writer of many hymns and poems of great beauty. She grew up in the Church of England, but later joined the Presbyterian Church of Scotland and became one of the staunch supporters of the Free Church Movement in that country. At the age of fifty, Anne married the Rev. William Cousin, a Scottish Presbyterian minister.

Mrs. Cousin became deeply engrossed with the writings of a great seventeenth-century Scottish Covenanter preacher, Samuel Rutherford, who was widely known as an outstanding evangelical preacher and one who strongly opposed the State Church of Scotland. His forceful preaching eventually caused his banishment to Aberdeen, where he was forbidden by the government to preach. During this period he wrote 220 letters of advice and encouragement to his pastorless flock at Anworth as well as to other nonconformist leaders in Scotland. These "prison epistles" have been termed "classics of devotion, counsel, and comfort." They established Rutherford as the most beloved writer of sacred literature during the seventeenth century.

Rutherford's exile ended in 1638 with the signing of the Solemn League and Covenant, the government's recognition of the independent church movement. He continued to be an influential leader among the nonconformists until 1660. Then once again—with the death of Cromwell, the end of the Commonwealth, and the restoration of Charles II—the wrath of the monarchy fell upon him. Rutherford was relieved of all of his offices and summoned to appear before the next British Parliament on charges of high treason. There was every likelihood that this would result in his being beheaded. The citation came too late, however, for Rutherford was already on his deathbed. His dying words were, "Glory, glory dwelleth in Immanuel's land." Two centuries later this triumphant statement became the inspiration for Anne Cousin's hymn text.

The hope of heaven during troubles is like the wind and sails to the soul. I wonder why a child of God would ever have a sad heart, considering what his Lord is preparing.

—Samuel Rutherford

In heav'n above, in heav'n above,
   God hath a joy prepared,
Which mortal ear hath never heard,
   nor mortal vision shared;
Which never entered mortal breast,
   by mortal lips was ne'er expressed,
'Tis God—the Lord of hosts!

—Laurentius Laurentil Laurinus
Trans. by William Maccall

He became poor that we might become rich (James 2:5).
He became a servant that we might become sons (Galatians 4:6-7).
He had no home that we might have a mansion in heaven (Matthew 8:20).
He was made sin that we might be made righteous (2 Corinthians 5:21).
He died that we might live eternally (John 5:24-25).

—Author Unknown

22

This World Is Not My Home

But our citizenship is in heaven. And we eagerly await a
Savior from there, the Lord Jesus Christ, who, by the
power that enables him to bring everything under his control,
will transform our lowly bodies so that they will
be like his glorious body.

—Philippians 3:20–21

This World Is Not My Home

Arr. by A. H. HOWARD, 1925–

Spiritual

1. This world is not my home, I'm just a pass-ing thru. My treas-ures
2. They're all ex-pect-ing me, and that's one thing I know, My Sav - ior
3. Just up in glo - ry - land we'll live e - ter - nal - ly, The saints on

are laid up some where be - yond the blue; The an - gels beck-on me from
par - doned me and now I on - ward go; I know He'll take me thru tho
ev - 'ry hand are shout-ing vic - to - ry, Their song of sweet-est praise drifts

heav-en's o - pen door,
I am weak and poor And I can't feel at home in this world an - y - more.
back from heav-en's shore

Refrain

O Lord, You know I have no friend like You, If

O Lord, You know, You know I have no friend like You, If

heav-en's not my home then Lord what will I do; The

heav - en's not my home, then Lord what will I do. The

I have a home above,
From sin and sorrow free,
A mansion which eternal love
Designed and formed for me.
—*Henry Bennett*

*A*s believers in Christ, we are transients in this world. Our real citizenship is in heaven. Each day finds us a little farther along the road to that eternal city "whose architect and builder is God" (Heb. 11:10).

The Scriptures teach that God "has . . . set eternity in the hearts of men" (Eccl. 3:11). We were destined to live eternally in fellowship with our heavenly Father. People in every culture believe that there is life after death and try to make provision for it. Throughout history this desire for immortality has resulted in many strange practices and beliefs, such as the ancient Egyptian preservation of the body or the modern fascination with reincarnation. For the Christian, however, the hereafter is centered in a Person, and the instructions for living eternally are clearly stated in God's holy Word. The stronger one's hope of glory, the greater becomes the homing desire for heaven. Reflecting on the anticipated "treasures laid up somewhere beyond the blue" only increases a discontent with this world.

I know not, O I know not
What joys await us there,
What radiancy of glory,
What bliss beyond compare.
—*Bernard of Cluny*
Trans. by John M. Neale

In her excellent book, *Heaven: Your Real Home,* published by the Zondervan Publishing House in 1995, Joni Eareckson Tada tells how the hope of heaven as expressed in this song has sustained her for the more than thirty years she has used a wheelchair. In 1967, as the result of a diving accident in the Chesapeake Bay, Joni suffered a broken neck that made her a quadriplegic. Yet to read her writings, hear her speak, admire her paintings done with a brush in her teeth, one senses quickly the glow of heaven that radiates from her life. Despite her disability, Joni travels around the world assisting other disabled persons and their families. She often states that after first seeing Christ, running and skipping down the golden streets of heaven is one of her cherished ambitions.

What a truth to contemplate: bodies that here have been stricken and twisted will there be transformed into the very likeness of our Savior's glorious body. And then, all of this life's unfulfilled dreams and cherished ambitions will be perfectly realized.

Lay hold on the hope set before you,
A hope that is steadfast and sure;
O haste to the blessed Redeemer,
The loving, the perfect and pure.
                                        —*Fanny J. Crosby*

Christians are not citizens of earth trying to get to heaven—but citizens of heaven making their way through the world.
                                        —*Vance Havner*

I have a future all sublime,
Beyond the realms of space and time,
Where my Redeemer I shall see
And sorrow nevermore shall be.
                                        —*N. Frykman*

23

We Shall See His Lovely Face

Father, I want those you have given me to be with me where I am, and to see my glory, the glory you have given me because you loved me before the creation of the world.

—John 17:24

We Shall See His Lovely Face

NORMAN J. CLAYTON, 1903–1992

NORMAN J. CLAYTON, 1903–1992

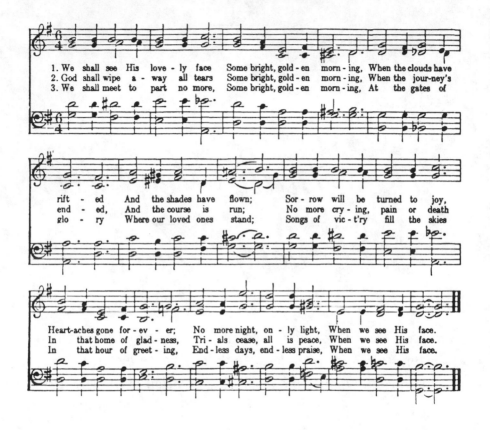

1. We shall see His love - ly face Some bright, gold - en morn - ing, When the clouds have rift - ed And the shades have flown; Sor - row will be turned to joy, Heart-aches gone for - ev - er; No more night, on - ly light, When we see His face.

2. God shall wipe a - way all tears Some bright, gold - en morn - ing, When the jour-ney's end - ed, And the course is run; No more cry - ing, pain or death In that home of glad - ness, Tri - als cease, all is peace, When we see His face.

3. We shall meet to part no more, Some bright, gold - en morn - ing, At the gates of glo - ry Where our loved ones stand; Songs of vic - t'ry fill the skies In that hour of greet - ing, End - less days, end - less praise, When we see His face.

I've seen the face of Jesus!
He smiled in love on me;
It filled my heart with rapture,
My soul with ecstasy.
Oh! glorious face of beauty,
Oh! gentle touch of care;
If here it is so blessed,
What will it be up there?
                    —*W. Spencer Walton*

Since earliest times the Christian church has taught that the ultimate bliss of heaven will be our total absorption with God. The initial experience in heaven of gazing on the face of Christ became known as the "Beatific Vision." This teaching has long been an important part of the church's study of eschatology—the doctrine of end-time events.

Norman J. Clayton, one of the talented and veteran gospel song writers of our time, captures this truth so well in this lovely gospel hymn. Clayton states that he composed the music while teaching himself to play the vibraharp. Later he added the text to fit the style of the music.

For much of his life, Mr. Clayton was involved in the building business as well as in his own music publishing company. For fifteen years Clayton was the organist with the Word of Life broadcasts and rallies in New York City. "We Shall See His Lovely Face" was first published in 1943, and several of his other well-known songs still in use include "Now I Belong to Jesus," "He Holds My Hand," and "My Hope Is in the Lord."

At the age of eighty-nine, Norman Clayton completed his earthly ministry and experienced the joy of everlasting life, a theme he had often used in his music:

For me He died, for me He lives,
And everlasting life and light He freely gives.
                    —*Norman J. Clayton*

Dr. E. Stanley Jones, evangelist and missionary statesman to India, was one day looking at Thorwaldsen's Statue of Christ, located in Copenhagen, Denmark. A Danish friend approached Dr. Jones and remarked, "You must first kneel at His feet in order to look into His face."

"So I knelt at His feet," recalls Dr. Jones, "and lo, His face was looking down into mine."

Kneel in worship before your Lord. Anticipate that moment in heaven when you will first behold His lovely face.

> I shall then with joy behold him,
> Face to face my Savior see;
> Fall with rapture and adore Him
> For His love to me.
>
> Nothing more shall then distress me
> In the land of sweet repose;
> Jesus stands engaged to bless me;
> This my Father knows.
> —*Mary S. B. Dana*

> One glimpse of His dear face all sorrow will erase,
> So bravely run the race till we see Christ.
> —*Esther Kerr Rusthoi*

God is trying to call us back to that for which He created us—to worship Him and to enjoy His presence forever.
—*A. W. Tozer*

Worship is an occupation, not with my personal needs or even with life's blessings, but with God Himself.
—*Author Unknown*

24

When I Get to Heab'n (Heaven)

And the ransomed of the LORD will return.
They will enter Zion with singing;
   everlasting joy will crown their heads.
Gladness and joy will overtake them,
   and sorrow and sighing will flee away.
—Isaiah 35:10

When I Get to Heab'n (Heaven)

Arr. by J. ROSAMOND JOHNSON, 1873–1954

Traditional Spiritual

vs. 3 I got a harp, you got a harp, all o' God's chillun got a harp; When I get to heab'n I'm goin' to take up my harp, I'm goin' to play all ovah God's Heab'n.

vs. 4 I got shoes, you got shoes, all o' God's chillun got shoes; When I get to heab'n I'm goin' to put on my shoes, I'm goin' to walk all ovah God's Heab'n.

vs. 5 I got a song, you got a song, all o' God's chillun got a song; When I get to heab'n, goin' to sing a new song, I'm goin' to sing all ovah God's Heab'n.

Ten thousand times ten thousand,
In sparkling raiment bright,
The armies of the ransomed saints
Throng up the steeps of light;
'Tis finished—all is finished—
Their fight with death and sin!
Fling open wide the golden gates,
And let the victors in.
                    —Dean Henry Alford

*I*n 1619 the first African natives landed at Jamestown, Virginia. This was the beginning of the slave trade in the American colonies. The succeeding years saw millions of Africans brought to this country, where they had to adapt to a new culture, learn a new language, and adjust to the cruel life of a slave. Yet out of this background came the songs we know as Negro spirituals, one of the finest bodies of folk music found anywhere in the world.

In the midst of their oppression, the slaves turned to the Christianity of white people and the hope it offered of heaven and the better life to come. The anticipation of heaven became one of the predominant themes of the slaves' many songs. Throughout their grievous existence, the slaves were sustained with the promise that, just as God had delivered the Israelites out of Egypt, He would one day give them liberation and freedom in heaven.

From 1871 to 1875 the Jubilee Singers of Fisk University toured the United States and Europe to introduce Negro spirituals to large audiences for the first time. In 1907, the songs first appeared in published form in Frederick J. Work's book, *Folk Songs of the American Negroes.*

Today in all cultures there is a growing appreciation of Negro spirituals. People of all races are realizing something of the nobleness and charm of these poignant expressions and are gaining a new awareness of the artistic genius of their black brothers and sisters.

To truly appreciate a Negro spiritual, one must deeply feel the truth of the music, realize something of the origin of the song, and sense keenly what the song must have meant in the lives of those who first sang it. These spirituals still reflect the religious attitudes and aspirations of many African-Americans.

> I want Jesus to walk with me;
> I want Jesus to walk with me;
> All along my pilgrim journey,
> Lord, I want Jesus to walk with me.
>
> In my trials, Lord, walk with me;
> In my trials, Lord, walk with me;
> When my heart is almost breaking,
> Lord, I want Jesus to walk with me.
>
> When I'm in trouble, Lord, walk with me;
> When I'm in trouble, Lord, walk with me;
> When my head is bowed in sorrow,
> Lord, I want Jesus to walk with me.
>
> *—Traditional spiritual*

Ev'ry body talkin' 'bout heab'n ain't goin' dere.

Only those who have been made alive with the eternal life of God while on earth will ever walk, fly, play, and sing "all over God's heaven."

> *Not everyone who says to me, "Lord, Lord," will enter the*
> *kingdom of heaven, but only he who does the will of my Father*
> *who is in heaven.*
>
> —Matthew 7:21

25

When We All Get to Heaven

After that, we who are still alive and are left will be caught up together with them in the clouds to meet the Lord in the air. And so we will be with the Lord forever. Therefore encourage each other with these words.

—1 Thessalonians 4:17–18

When We All Get to Heaven

ELIZA E. HEWITT, 1851–1920

EMILY D. WILSON, 1865–1942

1. Sing the won-drous love of Je-sus; Sing His mer-cy
2. While we walk the pil-grim path-way, Clouds will o-ver-
3. Let us then be true and faith-ful, Trust-ing, serv-ing
4. On-ward to the prize be-fore us! Soon His beau-ty

and His grace. In the man-sions, bright and bless-ed, He'll pre-
spread the sky; But when trav-'ling days are o-ver, Not a
ev-'ry day. Just one glimpse of Him in glo-ry Will the
we'll be-hold. Soon the pearl-y gates will o-pen; We shall

Refrain

pare for us a place.
shad-ow, not a sigh!
toils of life re-pay.
tread the streets of gold.
(1) for us a place.

When we all get to heav-en,
When we all get to heav-en,

What a day of re-joic-ing that will be! When we
What a day of re-joic-ing that will be!

all   see Je - sus, We'll sing and shout the vic - to - ry!

When we all see Je - sus, We'll sing and shout, and shout the vic - to-ry!

The light of heaven is Jesus' face,
The joy of heaven is Jesus' presence,
The harmony of heaven is Jesus' radiance,
The theme of heaven is Jesus' worth!

—*D. L. Moody*

There, from the music round me stealing,
I fain would learn the new and holy song,
And find at last, beneath Thy trees of healing,
The life for which I long.

—*John Greenleaf Whittier*

*A*llow your mind to anticipate the day. In the heavenly courts, the entire family of God—the redeemed from every tribe, language, people, and nation—will see their Lord and together will "sing and shout the victory." Think of mingling with Moses and Elijah as the three disciples did on the Mount of Transfiguration (Matt. 17:3), or imagine fellowshipping with the patriarchs, apostles, and saints of the ages. Anticipate the joyous reunion when husbands and wives, parents and children, and longtime friends meet there for the first time and recognize each other. "What a day of rejoicing that will be!"

Know each other? Blessed comfort!
When this mortal life is o'er,
We shall know our friends departed,
Kindred spirits gone before;
In our holy thrill of transport
They will be the first to share,
First to bid us joyous welcome—
We shall know each other there.

—*Fanny J. Crosby*

The author of this text, Eliza Edmunds Hewitt, was a schoolteacher in Philadelphia and a Christian lay worker who was deeply devoted to the Sunday school movement. Like many of the other gospel song writers during the latter half of the nineteenth century, Eliza's goal in writing her songs was to reach children and teach them the basic truths of the gospel. She dedicated this particular song to her own Sunday school class in Philadelphia. Though an invalid for much of her life, Eliza was always active and enjoyed a long personal friendship with Fanny Crosby. These two women met often for fellowship and discussion of their new hymns.

Miss Hewitt often attended the Methodist camp meetings at Ocean Grove, New Jersey. It was here that she collaborated with Emily Wilson, the wife of a Methodist district superintendent in Philadelphia, in the writing of this triumphant gospel hymn—a favorite of young and old alike. "When We All Get to Heaven" was first published in 1898.

O Lord,
    I live here as a fish in a vessel of water,
    Only enough to keep me alive;
    But in heaven I shall swim in the ocean.
    Here I have a little air in me to keep me breathing,
    But there I shall have sweet and fresh gales;
    Here I have a beam of sun to lighten my darkness,
    A warm ray to keep me from freezing;
    Yonder I shall live in light and warmth forever. Amen.
                —*A Puritan Prayer*

And let us consider how we may spur one another on toward love and good deeds. Let us not give up meeting together, as some are in the habit of doing, but let us encourage one another—and all the more as you see the Day approaching.
            —Hebrews 10:24–25

The Spirit and the bride say, "Come!" . . . Whoever is thirsty, let him come; and whoever wishes, let him take the free gift of the water of life.
            —Revelation 22:17

The House in My Future

—Buddy King

There's a house in my future, I have seen it in my dreams,
Surrounded by gardens and hedges—oh so green,
With rooms bathed in sunlight and hallways filled with joy,
And beautiful music resounding through its doors;
And this house is in heaven, Jesus promised it to me.

There's a house in my future, I have built it every day.
My God is my foundation, His Word shows me the way.
It's filled with love and mercy; it's built through prayer and faith,
And it's all held together by His amazing grace;
And this house is in heaven, Jesus promised it to me.

Thank you, Lord, for all the wondrous blessings
He's bestowed upon my life—and all He's given me.
Yet nothing can compare with the blessings
That await God's family through all eternity.
    And I pray you'll be my neighbor
    In that city bright and fair,
    If you'll just listen to my Savior—
    I know I'll meet you there.

And this house is in heaven, Jesus promised it to me;
And I'm living for the moment when I am finally free
To walk through gates of splendor with gold beneath my feet
To my house up in heaven, that
With my dying . . . will be complete!

(Sung by Diane King Susek and her brother, Buddy King, on Diane's CD and cassette tape "I Will Joy.") Used by permission.